Magic, Myth, and Mystery

VAMPIRES

DO YOU BELIEVE?

This series features creatures that excite our minds. They're magical. They're mythical. They're mysterious. They're also not real. They live in our stories. They're brought to life by our imaginations. Facts about these creatures are based on folklore, legends, and beliefs. We have a rich history of believing in the impossible. But these creatures only live in fantasies and dreams. Monsters do not live under our beds. They live in our heads!

45th Parallel Press

Published in the United States of America by Cherry Lake Publishing
Ann Arbor, Michigan
www.cherrylakepublishing.com

Reading Adviser: Marla Conn MS, Ed., Literacy specialist, Read-Ability, Inc.
Book Design: Felicia Macheske

Photo Credits: © Casther/Shutterstock.com, cover; © ArtThailand/Shutterstock.com, 1; © Lario Tus/
Shutterstock.com, 5; © Kiselev Andrey Valerevich/Shutterstock.com, 6, 9, 22; © Sadzak/Shutterstock.com,
11; © Andrey Bondarets/Shutterstock.com, 12; © Captblack76/Shutterstock.com, 15; © kasha_malasha/
Shutterstock.com, 17; © Daniel Brigginshaw/Shutterstock.com, 18; © Alina G/Shutterstock.com, 21;
© mountainpix/Shutterstock.com, 25; © udra11/Shutterstock.com, 27; © Ilona5555/Shutterstock.com, 28

Graphic Elements Throughout: © denniro/Shutterstock.com; © Libellule/Shutterstock.com; © sociologas/
Shutterstock.com; © paprika/Shutterstock.com; © ilolab/Shutterstock.com; © Bruce Rolff/Shutterstock.com

45th Parallel Press is an imprint of Cherry Lake Publishing.

Library of Congress Cataloging-in-Publication Data

Names: Loh-Hagan, Virginia, author.
Title: Vampires : magic, myth, and mystery / by Virginia Loh-Hagan.
Description: Ann Arbor : Cherry Lake Publishing, [2016] | Series: Magic,
 myth, and mystery | Includes bibliographical references and index.
Identifiers: LCCN 2016004923| ISBN 9781634711098 (hardcover) | ISBN
 9781634713078 (pbk.) | ISBN 9781634712088 (pdf) | ISBN 9781634714068 (ebook)
Subjects: LCSH: Vampires—Juvenile literature.
Classification: LCC GR830.V3 L64 2016 | DDC 398.21—dc23
LC record available at http://lccn.loc.gov/2016004923

Cherry Lake Publishing would like to acknowledge the work of The Partnership for 21st Century Skills.
Please visit www.p21.org for more information.

Printed in the United States of America
Corporate Graphics Inc.

TABLE of CONTENTS

Chapter One

Bloodsuckers

What are vampires? What are different types of vampires? What do vampires look like?

"I want to suck your blood." Vampires bite living things. Blood is their food.

Vampires were once human. They died. But they rose from the dead. They're **undead**. This means they're dead. But they act alive. They come out at night. They have "the hunger." They have the need to feed. They hunt for blood.

They kill animals. They kill humans. Human blood is the best. They also find **donors**. Donors are humans. They let vampires eat their blood.

Other undead creatures include mummies, ghosts, and zombies.

There are different types of vampires. **Dhampir** are half-vampire. And they're half-human. They're born. They have vampire powers. But they don't have vampire weaknesses. They become **slayers**. Slayers hunt vampires. They eat animal blood. They're rare.

Moroi are **mortal**. This means they can die. They're living vampires. They have vampire powers. They have magical powers. They live for 100 years. They're rare.

Strigoi are **immortal**. This means they live forever. They're evil. They're demons. They're the most dangerous. They're the most popular.

Most vampire stories are about strigoi.

Explained by Science!

Some people can't be in the sunlight. But they're not vampires. They may have xeroderma pigmentosum. It's known as XP. In extreme cases, they can't be exposed to sun and some lights. A few minutes can cause a lot of damage. People get XP as young children. They're called "children of the night." Their bodies can't repair skin damage. They get sunburns. They get blisters. They can get skin cancers. They can die. There's no known cure. It's rare. XP affects one in a million children in the United States. It affects one in 30,000 Navajo children. XP is six times more common in Japanese people. People with XP live in the dark. They wear clothes to cover their whole bodies. They wear sunscreen. They need special lighting. But they don't suck blood!

Many vampires sleep in coffins.

Vampires sleep in **havens**. Havens are their homes. They're dark places. Vampires live with **covens**. Covens are vampire groups. A coven has four vampires. They hunt together. There is a leader. He is the prince. A coven listens to a prince.

Vampires don't **decay**. Decay means rot. They keep their skin. Their skin is pale. It's a little blue. Vampires lose fat. They lose water. This makes their skin clear. Their veins can be seen. They stop growing hair. Their bodies are smooth. They're cold.

Chapter Two

Beware of the Fangs

What are the powers of vampires? Why are vampires good hunters?

Vampires bite. They bite necks. They bite other body parts. They have powerful **fangs**. Fangs are sharp teeth. They pierce skin. They're like tubes. Vampire blood is black. It has a **virus**. A virus is a sickness.

They have superpowers. They're stronger than 10 men. They're good fighters. They climb walls. They run fast. They jump high. They hear well. They smell well. They see well. They have **night vision**. They see in total darkness. They see heat. They track humans this way.

Vampire blood has a lot of iron. It carries more oxygen.

Vampires have long nails. They have thick nails.

Vampires have mind control. They read minds. They plant thoughts in humans' minds. They make humans do things. They have a magical gaze. They also control animals. They tell animals what to do. Some change into animals. They usually change into bats. Some change into wolves.

Vampires have super healing powers. They regrow their fangs. They regrow body parts. They don't get hurt easily. They don't get human sicknesses.

Vampires drink blood to heal themselves.

When Fantasy Meets Reality!

Candirus live in the Amazon river. They're called vampire fish. They're tiny catfish. They search for larger fish. They swim up into their gills. They feed on their blood. But there's more. Candirus are believed to attack humans. They like pee. Some people pee in the water. Candirus go to the pee. They enter humans through their private parts. They suck blood. They eat human tissue. They anchor themselves inside humans. They have spines. Their spines stick to humans' insides. They can't get out. They get stuck. They cause humans great pain. This may be just a legend. Many people believe it. But there's not much proof of candirus harming humans.

Vampires like to wear black.
Many wear long, black capes.

Vampires are hunters. They're powerful. They're smart. They're aware of everything. Humans can't sneak up on them. They don't get tired.

They're sneaky. They dress like humans. They act like humans. They blend in. They don't like attention. They don't like noise. They hunt quietly.

Some can become gas. They get into places. They get through door slits. They get through cracks. Some vampires can fly.

Chapter Three

Slaying Vampires

What are vampire weaknesses? How can vampires be harmed or killed?

Vampires are hard to kill. But they can be killed. Cutting off their head kills them. A **stake** through the heart kills them. Wooden stakes are pointy sticks. Slayers staked vampires to their coffins.

Vampires hate **holy** things. Holy refers to something religious. They hate holy water. They hate crosses. These things burn their skin.

Vampires have no soul. So they hate mirrors. They have no reflection. They have no shadow.

Vampires can't be on holy ground.

Vampires only need to be invited inside once.

They hate sunlight. Sunlight burns their skin. Vampires burst into flames. They turn to ashes.

They hate silver. Silver is pure. It burns them. But a lot of silver is needed to kill them.

They hate garlic. They have strong noses. Garlic has a strong smell. It keeps vampires away. But it doesn't kill them.

There are limits to their powers. They can't cross running water. Water is pure. Vampires have to be invited inside homes. They're evil. Humans have to allow evil in.

SURVIVAL TIPS!

- Get seeds or pebbles. Throw them around the door. This distracts vampires. Vampires have to count everything.

- Cut off a vampire's head. Use a silver blade. Keep the head away from the body. Otherwise, vampires can mend themselves back together. Boil the head in vinegar.

- Burn vampires. Make sure there are no remains. Eat the ashes.

- Make bread with vampire blood. Eat it.

- Avoid running into dark spaces or corners. Vampires like to trap their prey.

- Carry silver chains or silver handcuffs. Vampires can't break these.

- Bury vampires at a crossroads.

Getting Bit

**How do vampires make other vampires?
How do new vampires learn to be vampires?**

Vampires bite to feed. They suck out all the blood.
Most humans die. Sometimes, vampires don't let
humans die. They make new vampires. They bite.
They drink. They wait for humans to almost die.
They bite their own wrists. They let humans drink
their blood. Vampire blood is special. Humans die.
Then they become undead. They have vampire
blood in their bodies. They turn.

Turning is painful. It lasts three days. Humans get

sick. They get fevers. They get chills. They slip into a **coma**. A coma is a deep sleep. Some die. Some awaken as vampires. They're thirsty. They hunt right away.

Many humans are buried during the coma stage.
They come out of their graves as vampires

Vampires can't make babies. Turning is the only way to make new vampires. New vampires are **progeny**. This means children. They obey their **sires**. Sires are parents. They're the makers. They're the masters.

Newly created vampires are **fledglings**. They go through "the **becoming**." This is a process. They become full vampires. They learn from their sires. They learn from **elders**. Elders have been vampires for a long time. They share their knowledge. They teach hunting skills.

In some stories, vampires start out as "bags of blood."

Know the Lingo!

- **Alleycat:** a vampire without a home who sleeps in new places each day

- **Autovampirism:** drinking one's own blood

- **Banking:** taking blood from blood banks

- **Brood:** a group of vampires gathered around their leader

- **Butterfly:** a vampire who feeds only on the rich and famous

- **Childe:** an inexperienced vampire

- **Energy signature:** a special energy pattern that lets vampires find each other

- **Fallen to the beast:** losing control

- **Farmer:** a vampire who feeds on animals, not humans

- **Kindred:** fellow vampires

- **Kiss:** to drink human blood

- **Leech:** a bad word for vampire

- **Lupine:** werewolf

- **Seeker:** someone who wants to become a vampire

- **Vamp:** short for vampire

Chapter Five

Bad Bloodlines

Who were the first vampires? Who's Dracula?

Vampires were found in ancient cultures. Edimmu were demons. They weren't buried correctly. They came back from the dead. They sucked out humans' lives.

Ancient Egyptians had vampires. Sekhmet was a warrior goddess. She hunted humans. She killed them. She drank their blood. She had a nickname. It was the "Lady of the Bloodbath."

Ancient Greeks and Romans had vampires. Empusa hunted men. She waited for them to sleep. She sucked their blood. She ate their flesh.

Many cultures have vampire stories.

Real-World Connection

Maria Cristerna is "Vampire Lady." She has a world record. She's the female with the most body changes. She's the female with the most tattoos. She's covered in tattoos. The tattoos represent freedom. She said, "Warriors tattoo their faces." She inserted metal horns in her head. The horns represent strength. She added fangs into her gums. She has piercings. She has implants. She said, "I have always been very different. … I am expressing beauty through my art for the world to see." She's from Mexico. She was a lawyer. She has four children. She became a video jockey. She travels the world. A museum made a wax statue of her. She said, "It's my vampire dream to be immortal!"

Vampire stories are connected to religious stories.

Lilith is the mother of vampires. Her story is based on a Bible story. She was the first woman. She was Adam's first wife. Adam was God's son. Lilith didn't obey Adam. She thought they were equals. She was forced to leave. She became a demon. She had children. God sent angels to bring her back. She didn't want to go. She was punished. Her children were killed. She vowed to kill humans. She hunted humans. She drank their blood. She ate them.

The most famous vampire is Count Dracula. He was created by Bram Stoker. Count Dracula lives in Transylvania. He's based on a real person. He's based on Vlad Dracul.

Vlad killed over 100,000 people. He stuck them on poles. He put them around his castle. The **corpses** rotted. Corpses are dead bodies. He killed more people. He replaced the rotting bodies.

He nailed hats to heads. He skinned humans alive. He boiled them. He blinded them. He cut off body parts. He collected blood. He dipped bread into it. He was scarier than vampires!

Modern vampire stories came from Eastern European stories.

Did You Know?

- Mirrors used to be made of silver. That's another reason why vampires hate mirrors.

- Prince William may be related to Count Dracula (Vlad Dracul). His father told him, "Transylvania is in my blood."

- The Black Death killed many people in Europe. Vampires were blamed for causing plagues. Victims had blood coming out of their mouths. People thought they were vampires. They put rocks or bricks into their mouths. This was meant to stop vampires from coming back to life.

- Gravediggers and morticians reported corpses sitting up in their coffins. This spread the idea that vampires sleep in coffins.

- Vampires avoid children and babies. Their blood is pure. Their blood is poisonous to vampires. Dead human blood is also bad for vampires.

- Vampire bats eat blood. They have draculin in their spit. This stops blood from clotting.

- People were scared of vampires. So Europeans made laws. They created rules for burying the dead.

- Most vampires eat blood. But some don't. Some eat life forces. Some eat emotions. Emotions are feelings. Some eat souls. These vampires like crowds. They blend in. They take what they need.

Consider This!

Take a Position: Read about other undead creatures. (45th Parallel Press has a book about zombies.) Where do you rank vampires in regard to other undead creatures? Which undead creature is the scariest? Argue your point with reasons and evidence.

Say What? Read 45th Parallel Press's book about werewolves. Explain werewolves' strengths and weaknesses. Reread this book about vampires. Explain vampires' strengths and weaknesses. Which monster would win in a battle? Explain your reasoning.

Think About It! Vampires are everywhere. They're on television. They're in books. They're in movies. There seems to be more stories about vampires than other monsters. Why do you think people are so crazy about vampires? What makes vampires so interesting?

Learn More

- Gee, Joshua. *Encyclopedia Horrifica: The Terrifying Truth About Vampires, Ghosts, Monsters, and More.* New York: Scholastic, 2007.

- Hamilton, S. L. *Vampires.* Edina, MN: ABDO, 2011.

- Jenkins, Mark Collins. *Vampires: Unearthing the Legend.* Washington, DC: National Geographic, 2012.

- Klepeis, Alicia Z. *Vampires: The Truth Behind History's Creepiest Bloodsuckers.* Edina, MN: Capstone Press, 2015.

Glossary

becoming (bih-KUHM-ing) process of changing from fledgling to full vampire

coma (KOH-muh) deep sleep caused by trauma

corpses (KORPS-iz) bodies of dead people

covens (KOH-vinz) vampire groups

decay (dih-KAY) to rot

dhampir (DAHM-peer) half-vampire and half-human

donors (DOH-nurz) people who voluntarily let vampires drink their blood

elders (EL-durz) old vampires that are leaders

fangs (FANGZ) sharp teeth that suck blood from a body

fledglings (FLEJ-lingz) newly created vampires

havens (HAY-vuhnz) vampire homes

holy (HOH-lee) connected to religion

immortal (ih-MOR-tuhl) living forever

moroi (mo-ROY) mortal vampires

mortal (MOR-tuhl) not able to live forever

night vision (NITE VIZH-uhn) the ability to see in darkness

progeny (PRAH-jeh-nee) vampire children

sires (SYE-urz) parents

slayers (SLAY-urz) people, sometimes dhampirs, who hunt and kill vampires

stake (STAYK) sharp wooden stick

strigoi (STREH-goy) immortal vampires

undead (un-DED) creatures that were dead and brought back to life

virus (VYE-ruhs) sickness

Index

About the Author

Dr. Virginia Loh-Hagan is an author, university professor, former classroom teacher, and curriculum designer. She keeps vampire hours. She works at night. She sleeps during the day. She lives in San Diego with her very tall husband and very naughty dogs. To learn more about her, visit www.virginialoh.com.